Written by Kenman Wong and Donovan Richards

Graphic Design and Layout by University Communications, Seattle Pacific University

Published by:
Seattle Pacific University Center for Integrity in Business
3307 Third Avenue West
Seattle, WA 98119
cib@spu.edu
206-281-2502

ISBN 978-1725863828

FAITH & CO.

BUSINESS ON PURPOSE

Introduction

Developed by a team of educators, filmmakers and business leaders at Seattle Pacific University, *Faith & Co: Business on Purpose* seeks to inspire and equip you to live out your faith at work. Used in conjunction with a series of short films, this guide is meant to facilitate whole life discipleship through formational group interaction around the theme of joining God's work of redeeming all things, including the marketplace.

To view the film resources in this study guide, please go to:

www.faithand.co and follow the link to "Study Guide."

Note: Viewing the videos from a web-enabled ("smart") television works best. In the absence of one, we recommend connecting your television to your device using an HDMI cable or a mirroring device like Chromecast (Google Cast), Apple Airplay, Roku Streaming Stick, or Amazon Fire TV.

Faith & Co: Business on Purpose Group Study Guide

Overview

It's a rare occurrence for Christian business people to hear a sermon that affirms their work as spiritually significant. Instead, the indirect message we receive is that the only way to serve God at work is by sharing our faith with co-workers or by giving money to support churches and/or missionaries serving in faraway places. In other words, business only has *instrumental* value for eternal purposes. In contrast, the tasks we perform every day (i.e., planning, designing, managing) and the actual products and/or services we make or provide are only incidental to God's care and concern.

As a result, many of us are burdened with a deep disconnect between our work and our spiritual lives. We put in long hours (over 90,000 across a lifetime) without a sense that the work we actually do matters to God. We are also left without substantive guidance on how our faith should make a difference with respect to *why* and *how* we do our work. As a result, our lives become compartmentalized as our faith ends up having little bearing upon the place where we spend the bulk of our time and energy.

"Business is not a necessary evil. It's much more accurate to say that it's a necessary channel of redemption in a broken world." Bruce Baker

---

Based upon the biblical conviction that Christ's mission is to reconcile all things (Col. 1:20), *Faith & Co: Business on Purpose* invites you to deepen your faith and to experience whole life discipleship by developing a scripturally informed approach to business. Through films, interviews, exercises, and conversation, you will learn how every part of your life, especially working in the messy world of business, can be an avenue for worshipping God and serving your neighbor.

Our hope and prayer is that you will no longer see business as only a necessary evil, but that you can begin to re-imagine it as a necessary channel of God's redemption and reconciliation of all things.

JOURNAL:

Part 1: Foundations

The first part of this study (Phases 1–5) will focus on foundations. These phases will develop an understanding of business through the Creation, Fall, Redemption, and New Creation narrative arc of Scripture. Biblical core values (ethics) and work as a place for spiritual formation will also be explored.

Phase 1

Introduction to Faith & Co.

Introduction to Faith & Co.

Approach (5 minutes)

This study guide is meant to be used as a group discipleship resource in conjunction with Seattle Pacific University's short film series, *Faith & Co: Business on Purpose.* This series, filmed across the globe, features stories of leaders in a wide range of industries who are living out their faith in the marketplace. Utilizing these films along with additional interviews with subject matter experts, this study will develop a biblically informed understanding of business as a calling to serve God and love our neighbors and explore implications for why and how we do our work.

This 10-week study covers:

Foundations

> Phase 1: Introduction and How to Use This Study Guide
>
> Phase 2: Business as a Calling
>
> Phase 3: Business in the Messy Middle
>
> Phase 4: Ethics and Core Values
>
> Phase 5: Spiritual Formation

Right Relationships

> Phase 6: The Workplace as a Redemptive Community
>
> Phase 7: Customers: Re-Personalizing the Marketplace
>
> Phase 8: Business and Flourishing Communities
>
> Phase 9: Creation Care
>
> Phase 10: Next Steps

Each week's lesson ("Phase") follows an approximately 90-minute template that can be adjusted as necessary. If you have only 60 minutes, the main story and reflections films or exercises should be enough to carry the discussion each week. Since we cannot anticipate the size or participation level of groups using this guide, we strongly encourage leaders to preview each week's materials to make any necessary adjustments. Your time will be divided between watching short videos, discussion, application exercises, reflection, and prayer. Videos should take no more than 30 to 40 minutes of the group's time and the rest should be dedicated to reflection, discussion, and prayer.

▶ WATCH

The short videos are divided between stories that focus on specific individuals, reflections ("Thinking out Loud") by business leaders and "Going Deeper" interviews with subject matter experts. *All of the video content can we found at www.faithand.co. Please click on the "Study Guide" section.*

💬 DISCUSSION

In this guide, a handful of questions for each film have been developed to facilitate group discussion. Some questions might feel personal and there is no requirement to answer every question. But it is often helpful to open up and be vulnerable in group settings. Sometimes, answering God's call on your life means engaging in heartfelt discussion. In order to allow vulnerability, it is important for everyone in the group to be considerate and respectful of each other and accepting of alternate points of view. We strongly encourage leaders to act as facilitators in order to create a climate in which all participants feel free to share.

‖–‖ EXERCISES

Each week, the study guide provides exercise prompts. These prompts require more thinking and are forward-focused. The idea behind the exercises is to encourage you to think about ways of applying these ideas into daily life habits. The hope is that these exercises will help you create action-oriented goals to translate the ideas from this study into tangible behavior at work.

✎ REFLECTION AND PRAYER

The study guide also provides prompts for prayer. At times, when Christians are gathered, moments of reflection and an openness to prayer can lead to inspiration. Feel free to pray the prayers included in the guide, or use the timelines to pray in whatever way is most comfortable for your group.

Additional resources

Leaders preparing to use this guide and/or persons interested in learning more about these topics are encouraged to enroll in Seattle Pacific University's free online course on the topic: www.faithand.co. You will also find references to additional resources (books, articles, organizations) in the appendix of this guide.

This study is intended for business people, students, ministry professionals and anyone interested in learning more about the connections between Christian faith and business. The goals are to inspire, challenge, and equip you to re-imagine what business could be.

However, the terms "faith" and "business" can have a variety of meanings, especially when they are used in conjunction. The following are a few points of clarification about what this study is (and is not):

1. The aim is to point you toward faithful living. While many biblically informed practices may lead to higher profits, faithfulness is the primary goal.

2. While attempting to include a broad spectrum of denominations and traditions, we hope to steer clear of tacitly reinforcing the prosperity gospel. The Bible never promises that faithfulness will lead to material blessings. In contrast, obedience can be costly.

3. The film subjects are meant serve as faithful expressions, rather than definitive models. They are intended to portray *a* (vs. *the*) Christian way to embody faithfulness. Some of the films and/or interviews may spark controversy and some debate. This is something to be encouraged. Honest conversation and deep learning take place amid tension and multiple perspectives.

4. Most of the films are about people who have high degrees of power in their organizations, but *everyone* has a sphere of influence. Within Christ's upside-down kingdom, even small or invisible acts can be significant (i.e., the story of the widow's mite). So even if you are not (or not yet) a leader, you may be able to effect changes on a smaller, but equally significant, scale (i.e., with the person in the neighboring cubicle, a customer, or with a product, process, or service you help design or revamp).

5. This guide explores the intersections of Christian theology and business. It is not a study of comparative religious approaches. Nor is it meant to be an exercise in triumphalism. Since all that is good, true, and beautiful comes from God, we should not be surprised to find that Christians are not the only people engaged in re-imagining the marketplace. We have every reason to exercise humility as we are joining God's work rather than doing it by ourselves.

💬 DISCUSS (50 MINUTES)

- Share your work history. What do you currently do? Describe the journey that led to your current place.

- Do you believe you are called to your current work or place in life? Why or why not?

- Do you believe Christians should bring their faith to work? If so, what does this look like? What are appropriate and inappropriate ways to integrate faith and work?

- What are the hot topics at you workplace? How prepared do you feel about speaking Christian wisdom into those topics?

- How helpful has your church been in preparing you to integrate your faith and your work?

📖 READ

Here is a brief preview of some of the stories we will experience and topics we will discuss in the weeks ahead

▶ WATCH (1 MINUTE)

Phase 1, Film 1: Faith & Co. Trailer

✏ PRAY/JOURNAL (5 MINUTES)

Heavenly Father, Thank you for your provision and for your love. Thank you for providing us all with a time to consider your truth thoughtfully within the context of our work. May you open our hearts and minds to the story you are trying to tell through our work over these next 10 weeks. May we be receptive to the call you are giving us and may we encourage each other toward purposeful work. Amen.

▮▮ EXERCISE (10 MINUTES)

As you think about the topics we will discuss over the next 10 weeks, what do you hope to get out of this series?

_____

_____

_____

_____

_____

The Calling and Purpose of Business

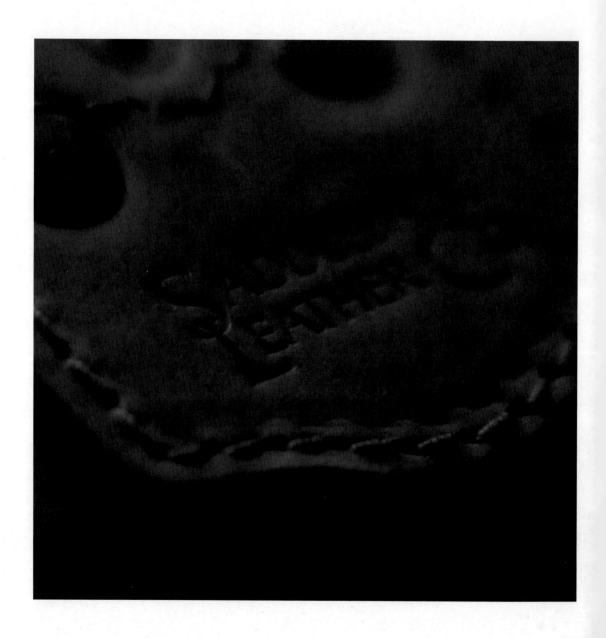

The Calling and Purpose of Business

Introduction (5 minutes)

"What do you do?"

This question opens most social introductions. Whether at church, a mixer, or on adjacent airplane seats, once two strangers meet and exchange names, the first question is usually about occupation. That's to be expected, considering the amount of time and energy we devote to work. We spend 40+ hours per week (about 90,000 over a lifetime) working to pay bills, provide sustenance, and enjoy ourselves if there's anything left over.

Despite the prevalence of work in our lives, the instruction we receive on Sundays tends to be disconnected from what we do come Monday. In fact, churches often devalue the work of their members by passing down a spiritual hierarchy in which "full-time ministry" occupies the top, helping professions such as health care and teaching make up the middle, and business sits squarely at the bottom. Christians involved in business can serve God by sharing the gospel with co-workers and by earning money to support ministries and missions work. However, day-to-day responsibilities like designing products, brand strategy, setting up supply chains, managing, and selling are dismissed as incidental to one's faith.

What would it look like to describe "what you do" with more than a quick sentence or your job title? What if you could speak about how your work is more than an economic exchange, but is a calling to serve God's purposes in the world?

This phase focuses on the first movement of the Creation, Fall, Redemption, and New Creation narrative arc of Scripture and aims at helping you develop a biblical perspective or a theology of business by exploring the following questions:

- Can Christian business people be confident that God sees their work as being just as spiritually significant as full-time ministry within the church?

- Does God have unique purposes, or a calling, for business? If so, what are those purposes and how do they fit God's plans?

- Is *how* we do our work a spiritual matter? Beyond being a bit kinder and more honest, are decisions like determining which markets to enter, how to pay employees, and how we market our goods and services within the realm of God's care and concern?

Story: Saddleback Leather Company

"Everything God does is quality. No exceptions."

📖 READ

To begin to develop a biblical perspective on business, let's meet Dave and Suzette Munson, owners of Saddleback Leather Company. Dave founded the company "by accident" while serving as a missionary in Mexico. Initially, Dave struggled with reconciling his sense of calling to do ministry with owning and operating a business.

▶ WATCH: (10 MINUTES)

Phase 2, Video 1: "Not Dead Yet" (Saddleback Leather Company)

💬 DISCUSS (15 MINUTES):

- Can you make a biblical/theological case to support Dave's (and Suzette's) journey to seeing owning a business as a ministry?

- While business can indeed serve *instrumental* purposes (i.e., evangelism, earning money to support ministries), is there anything *intrinsic* to the work of Saddleback Leather Co. that might also matter to God and align with kingdom purposes?

> In addition to sharing the gospel and financially supporting missions and other humanitarian organizations, Saddleback delights customers with beautiful, quality products backed by an eye-popping limited 100-year warranty. It creates economic opportunity in Leon, Mexico and treats all employees with respect. All these aspects of business matter to God, who seeks to redeem all creation, including all corners of culture and every relationship.

✏ PRAY/JOURNAL (5 MINUTES)

Heavenly Father, thank you for your love. Thank you for creating a world of beauty and quality. I pray that you open my heart to the opportunities you have given me in my life to do things that are beautiful and full of quality. May my work be an exhibit Reflections: to your love. Amen.

Write out what you believe God's call on your life might be

_____

_____

_____

_____

_____

_____

Reflections

▶ WATCH (2 MINUTES)

Phase 2 Video 2: Steve Bell (:40)

Phase 2 Video 3: Hans Hess (1:29)

💬 DISCUSS (15 MINUTES)

- Can you relate to Steve and Hans' experiences or the conceptions of work that created tensions for them? What theological assumptions about work/business do you bring to your understanding of vocational significance and/or direction?

- What would you say to someone facing questions like Steve and Hans did earlier in their lives?

Going Deeper

Let's begin developing a Biblical/theological understanding of business by looking to the creation movement within Scripture's "big story."

▶ WATCH (6 MINUTES)

Phase 2 Video 4: Jeff Van Duzer – "Why Business Matters to God" (6:02)

> **All work can participate in God's mission of the redemption and reconciliation of all things:**
>
> - In Genesis, the fall alienates humans from God, their own sense of self, each other, and everything around them.
>
> - The larger narrative and specific passages (i.e., Romans 8:19-21) of Scripture point to eventual redemption of all that is broken, including the material world and human culture.
>
> - In Luke 4, Jesus reads from Isaiah to declare his public ministry (good news to the poor, etc.). The "year of the Lord's favor" refers to the Jubilee, where debts were cleared, slaves were set free, and the land was given a sabbatical.
>
> - Col. 1:4 states that God is redeeming all things through Christ.

Story: Hill Country Memorial

"What I do pushes back against death, brokenness, and disease."

📖 READ

Let's watch as Emily Padula, Chief Strategy Officer at Hill Country Memorial Hospital, a health care system in Fredricksburg, Texas, tells her story and demonstrates how a vocational framework can enhance meaning and motivation and influence the direction of an institution.

▶ WATCH (5 MINUTES)

Phase 2 Video 5: "Remarkable Always" (Hill Country Memorial)

💬 DISCUSS (15 MINUTES):

- How does Emily's story inform your view of God's purpose for your work?

- Can you describe ways in which your work serves as a foretaste or signpost to God's eventual healing and redeeming of the world? How would you describe God's concern for your daily activities?

✏️ PRAY/JOURNAL (5 MINUTES)

Heavenly Father, thank you for your vision to see the world as whole. Thank you for inspiring Emily and Hill Country Memorial to work diligently toward pushing back death, brokenness, and disease. I pray that you would open my eyes to the opportunities you have placed before me and the ways I can use those opportunities to help other people thrive.

‖–‖ EXERCISE

No matter your occupation, even if your work is largely hidden and goes unnoticed, your work matters to God.

Below, write down three things you can do to fulfill God's purpose for your work tomorrow. Spend this week praying about how you can be purposeful about these three items during your daily work.

_____

_____

_____

_____

_____

Further Reflections (optional)

To hear how others connect their work and their faith, please watch the following videos:

Phase 2:

Video 6: Marta Norton Klock (1:18)

Video 7: Sonny Vu (2:47)

Video 8: John Marsh (1:45)

Video 9: Don Flow (2:47)

🔥 KEY TAKEAWAYS (5 MINUTES)

3 Models

There are 3 primary approaches to connecting faith and work.

1. The first is a Dualistic approach, or what might be enacted as "Business is Business"

2. The second is the Instrumental model, often characterized as "Business as Mission"

3. The third approach sees faith and work/ business as integral/intrinsic. We might call this "Business is Mission."

Business is Mission emphasizes:

- Work was always God's intention and is an important way to participate in God's ongoing creation and care and provision for all.

- Business matters to God and is a calling/vocation equivalent to "full-time ministry."

- Business advances God's purposes in the world by bringing order out of chaos, and by providing goods and services and creating meaningful work for people.

- If we are to do our work under God's direction, why and how we do our work matters greatly.

How might I view or approach business differently if I view it as integral to God's mission?

_____

_____

_____

_____

Phase 3

Business in the Messy Middle

Business in the Messy Middle

Introduction (5 minutes)

"How was work today?"

Such a simple question often prompts outpourings of frustration and pain. How did this come to be? Genesis teaches that God worked and delighted in it, created us to do the same, and entrusted us with a substantial role in his ongoing work in the world. Why, then, is our labor sometimes arduous, strife-ridden, and full of limits and trade-offs between what we *should* and what we *can* do (i.e., price vs. quality, higher wages vs. lower prices, truth telling vs. gaining a sale)?

While all types of work can be vocations that help accomplish God's purposes in the world, it's important to avoid either romanticizing work (and business) as wholly good or dismissing it as irreparably broken.

In this phase, we will continue developing a theology of business by exploring what the other biblical movements (Fall, Redemption, New Creation) have to say about our work. More specifically, we will explore why work and the general human condition can be characterized by "thistles and thorns." We will also learn why we have good reason to be hopeful rather than cynical amid the broken realities we experience.

Following the Creation account (Genesis 1-2), the rest of the major movements of the Bible address three big questions:

1. What's wrong with the world and the human condition?

2. What's God doing to repair and redeem it?

3. What should we do in response?

Reflections

▶ WATCH (5 MINUTES TOTAL)

Phase 3 Video 1: Chi-En Yu (2:53)

Phase 3 Video 2: Hans Hess (2:15)

DO YOU SEE THE IMAGE OF GOD IN OTHERS?

💬 DISCUSS (15 MINUTES)

Like Chi-En and Hans, where do you most keenly feel the brokenness of the world and/or the gap between what you should and can do? Where do you wish for a third way to appear?

Going Deeper

Let's explore how the Bible addresses these questions and their implications for our work. We'll begin by looking at biblical teaching on what's wrong with the world and why the human condition and our work can feel so broken and frustrating.

▶ WATCH (5 MINUTES)

Phase 3 Video 3: Jeff Van Duzer, "The Fall's Effect on our Work." (3:22)

💬 DISCUSS (10 MINUTES)

- What do you make of the idea of accepting limits, and seeing the Fall as our desire to be limitless?

- How and where do you experience limits and/or the desire to be limited in your work?

Story: Marsh Collective

"There's hope for people that are broken; there's beauty in broken things."

📖 READ

Let's watch the story about a couple for whom the themes of hope and redemption are central despite deep brokenness in their own lives and in their community. John and Ashley Marsh are the owners of Marsh Collective, a group of businesses based in Opelika, Alabama.

▶ WATCH (10 MINUTES)

Phase 3 Video 4: "Beauty out of Brokenness"

💬 DISCUSS (20 MINUTES)

- What do you think of the Marshes' story? How does it testify to God's redemptive work?

- How might you participate in God's redemptive work and bring hope to others through your work? You might think that such redemptive work only matters at an executive level, but people can make a difference no matter the role.

- What small changes can you make to shift your work toward a redemptive focus?

Going Deeper

Redemption/ New Creation

📖 READ

The Fall is a painful continuation of the biblical story with far-reaching consequences. However, it's only a placeholder in the overall narrative. A myopic focus on it leaves us unduly pessimistic and can tempt us toward cynicism. The good news is that the remaining parts of the story (from early Genesis onward) are about God's redemptive mission to make things right again, and how we can join in these endeavors.

The Marshes see their work as participating in the redemptive work of God. Let's explore biblical teaching about why this perspective on work is necessary and why our efforts are meaningful for eternity.

▶ WATCH (3 MINUTES)

> Phase 3 Video 5: Jeff Van Duzer, "The End of the Story: Redemption & New Creation" (3:14)

💬 DISCUSS

- How does marinating in the images of the end of the story help erase doubts about your work and its meaning for eternity?

- How does fixing and building relate to your work/business?

✏️ PRAY/JOURNAL (10 MINUTES)

Heavenly Father, thank you for the redemption you have orchestrated in the lives of John and Ashley Marsh. Thank you for the work you are doing to redeem our private lives and the work you are doing to redeem our communities. Please help me cooperate with you as you engage in your redemptive work in me, and guide me in the ways I might act in redemptive work in the messy middle of my community. Amen.

‖–‖ EXERCISE

We don't need to look far to see brokenness in this world. No matter where we live, broken and hurt people comprise much of our community. Whether addressing issues of homelessness, job losses, opioid addiction, or broken relationships, we all have an opportunity to be in the restoration business through our work.

Write down a few ideas for how you can restore your community this week.

_____

_____

_____

_____

Further Reflections (5 minutes, Optional)

To learn more about how business leaders live into God's redemptive mission, watch a selection of these "Thinking out Loud" videos:

Phase 3 Videos 6-10:

Video 6: Chi-Ming Chien (1:59)

Video 7: Erik Lokkesmoe (1:01)

Video 8: Steve Bell (0:31)

Video 9: Eric Stumberg (0:45)

Video 10: Don Flow (0:24)

🔥 KEY TAKEAWAYS (5 MINUTES)

- Living in the messy middle means that we should expect frustration and tension in our work.

- After the Fall, work that repairs something broken and/or gives a glimpse of life as it could be became necessary.

- Because God will redeem all things in the end, we can take a longer perspective to see beyond the trials and tribulations of our work.

- We do not work alone. Our work is enabled by the Holy Spirit even amid difficult decisions.

- No matter our job title, we all have a sphere of influence where we can be faithful and redemptive.

How might I go about participating in God's redemptive work by repairing broken things and/or by giving glimpses or being a signpost of what's to come while living in the messy middle?

_____

_____

_____

_____

_____

_____

Phase 4

Ethics and Core Values

Ethics and Core Values

Introduction (5 minutes)

"If we pull the trigger, we can make a lot of money."

Have you ever heard a phrase like this one? It feels like it happens all the time, business people strategizing about maximizing returns. But, when the business case overrides all other considerations, unethical behavior might be right around the bend. Tragic and frequent headlines are reminders that the opportunity to make more money may mean cutting corners in legal, but ethically questionable, ways.

In the first two phases, we've come to see how the marketplace can advance God's mission of reconciliation and redemption. We are promised that, in the end, it all works out according to God's purposes. Yet, for now, we live in the messy middle, so we can expect to face decisions that present us with dimensions of right and wrong, have competing interests, and can't be easily resolved. For example, how much should we reveal to a client if he or she doesn't ask? How far is too far when gathering and using data to gain insights into our customers? Acting in God-pleasing ways in these situations requires wisdom, guidance, and discernment, some of the central concerns of Christian ethics.

In this phase, we will explore how the Bible can and should be used to guide our business decisions. Since most of us work with colleagues from a wide variety of (or no) faith traditions, we will also look at the issue of translating Biblical ethics to pluralistic contexts.

Given the limits imposed by living in the messy middle, it's tempting to turn business into a game to be played by its own rules, making business ethics an oxymoron. Conversely, many of us have been taught that good ethics really is just good business. In other words, ethical behavior makes strategic sense as it's in our best long-term financial interest. Let's begin by considering some reasons why ethics should be of special concern to Christians, and the relationship between ethics and profitability.

Reflections

▶ WATCH (3 MINUTES)

Phase 4 Video 1 Eric Stumberg (1:10)

Phase 4 Video 2 Jeff Van Duzer, "Oxymoron or Good Business" (1:18)

💬 DISCUSS

- While it's tempting to think that business is business, an area of our lives that is cordoned off from the gospel, discuss a theological implication of a business decision you've recently made.

- Share an experience in which doing the right thing was costly.

⏸ EXERCISE (10 MINUTES)

📖 READ

- Leviticus 19:35-36

- Deuteronomy 24:15

- Proverbs 11:3

- Isaiah 58:3

- Colossians 3:23-4

💬 DISCUSS:

- What do these passages tell us about how God values our behavior in business?

- Describe an issue you have faced at work where the Bible seems unclear or silent.

- Where should we turn for guidance if the Bible is unclear or silent, or when a relevant passage seems context bound (i.e., Old Testament prohibitions on charging interest on a loan)?

The point of this exercise is to demonstrate the limits of prooftexting and/or using the Bible as a rulebook. While the Bible does have much to say about our behavior in all areas of our lives, some commands are context-bound and many contemporary business issues are not *directly* addressed. However, we can still find guidance in the Bible and allow it to speak into our lives if we look beyond commands to its many forms of moral instruction (i.e., parables, wisdom literature, letters, history, etc.), its larger story, and broader paradigms or core values.

Our primary task in reading Scripture should be less about finding specific rules than it is to find out who God is and what he cares about. In so doing, we are being formed to look through the Bible and interact with the world through its assumptions, metaphors, and priorities. In conjunction with Scripture, we also have the Holy Spirit and the wisdom and discernment of fellow believers to help guide us.

Story: Flow Motors

"Faith is something we exercise; it is not an abstract concept. Love is something we actually live."

📖 READ

Let's watch a highly inspiring film about Don Flow and his leadership at Flow Companies Inc. Flow has thoughtfully contextualized and deeply integrated Biblical values – especially the larger narrative and core values – in order to reimagine what car sales and repair might look like in light of the redemptive arc of Scripture.

▶ WATCH (7 MINUTES)

Phase 4 Video 3: "Driving Trust" (7 minutes)

💬 DISCUSS (20 MINUTES)

- What do you think of Don Flow's story? Can an honest car dealer thrive, or even survive?

- How can you draw from the larger narrative of the Bible to inform your work?

- A significant part of ethical behavior is preparation and alignment. How can you best prepare yourself and/or your organization to avert crisis and to act in a redemptive direction?

✏ PRAY/JOURNAL (10 MINUTES)

Heavenly Father, thank you for the promises you have provided in the narrative of Scripture. Thank you for the work you are doing at Flow Motors. I pray for guidance around how I might interpret the values you have placed in Scripture for my specific work setting. Guide me in ways that I can live your core values and good ethics on a daily basis. Amen.

Write down a list of Biblical values you can live daily at your work.

_____

_____

_____

_____

_____

_____

Going Deeper

▶ WATCH (3 MINUTES)

Let's watch Dr. Bruce Baker, associate professor of business ethics at Seattle Pacific University, for insight on how we should appropriately use the Bible for ethical guidance. Using language that's common in business, he elucidates Biblical core values that can guide our business decisions.

> Phase 4 Video 4: Bruce Baker on Biblical Core Values (3:19)

💬 DISCUSS (10 MINUTES)

- Where do grace, soul, and shalom already appear in your work?

- How might your work or decisions change in light of grace, soul, and shalom?

📖 READ (3 MINUTES)

One significant challenge of living out our faith in the marketplace is the fact that we live in highly pluralistic contexts, so we have to learn how to thoughtfully translate our ideas to others who don't share our beliefs.

Don Flow is an thoughtful exemplar. He and his employees deconstructed every part of the business and re-imagined and rebuilt it according to redemptive values. Yet people of all sorts of (and no) faith commitments are employed at Flow. Part of his success has been the ability to translate Biblical values into broadly acceptable language and practices. For example, neighbor love can be translated into "how do I treat a customer as I would a guest in my home?" Flourishing/shalom can translated into the idea of "a polis" (a thriving community where all types of capital grow).

Translating Christian ethics is a challenging task. Some things will not translate into profitable business formulas. Yet because every person is made in the image of God, aspects of his purposes, character, and will resonate across cultures and beliefs. As Don Flow illustrates in his leadership at Flow Companies, the process of developing a "lived theology" is ongoing but doing so brings meaning to the larger story of God's redemptive work.

Reflections (5 minutes)

To learn more about the challenges and opportunities of translation, watch all or some of the following videos:

▶ WATCH

> Phase 4 Video 4: Steve Garber (1:03)

> Phase 4 Video 5: Ron Johnson (1:38)

Phase 4 Video 6 Don Flow (:38)

Phase 4 Video 7 Sonny Vu (:57)

💬 DISCUSS:

- How could you go about translating Christian values in your work?

- Are there limits to the biblical values that can be translated into business? If so, what are those limits?

_____

_____

_____

_____

_____

_____

Further Reflections (optional)

To learn more about how Biblical ethics can be applied to the marketplace, watch the following "Thinking out Loud" videos:

- Phase 4 Video 8: Chi-En Yu (1:41)

- Phase 4 Video 9: Marta Norton Klock (0:50)

🔥 KEY TAKEAWAYS

- In using the Bible for ethical guidance, our primary task is to see through it by reading it to learn about who God is and what he cares about.

- The Bible should not be reduced to a user's manual or rulebook.

- The Bible employs many types of moral instruction (including stories, paradigms, core values, proverbs, history) and requires careful interpretation within a community of the faithful.

- Translating/contextualizing Christian ethics is a challenging task. Not everything will translate well. Yet because every person is made in the image of God, some aspects of his purposes, character, and will resonate across cultures, contexts, and worldviews.

Phase 5

Spiritual Formation

Spiritual Formation

Introduction (5 minutes)

Conversations about faith at work usually move in the direction of the influence we hope to have on our places of employment (i.e., *bringing* our faith to work). Far less frequently discussed is how our work shapes us (for better or worse) and how God might use what we do as an academy for our spiritual maturation.

When we do connect spiritual formation to work, we often resort to classic disciplines that are practiced *alongside* our employment. We pray and read Scripture. We tithe and try to regularly observe Sabbath. These are important disciplines, but we often overlook opportunities for spiritual growth presented by the work itself. In his book, *Christ Plays in Ten Thousand Places: A Conversation in Spiritual Theology,* Eugene Peterson states, "I'm prepared to contend that the primary location for spiritual formation is in the workplace."

Work plays a significant role in our spiritual development because it is a place where we spend much of our time (about 90,000 hours over a lifetime). Whether or not we are aware of it, what we do all day forms (or *mal-*forms) us. Every interaction we have and decision we make has the effect of a character/soul shaping liturgy. The number of hours we work, our response to a co-worker during a tense meeting and our approach to designing products and marketing strategies shape who we're becoming. The only real question is whether our hearts are being formed toward or away from Christ's kingdom.

In *Renovation of the Heart: Putting on the Character of Christ,* Dallas Willard describes spiritual formation as "the Spirit-driven process of forming the inner world of the human self in such a way that it becomes like the inner being of Christ himself." Intentional disciplines, practices, and postures, both in *and* alongside our work, make space for the Spirit to work in our lives. Much in the way that an athlete or an apprentice needs repetition to master a skill, spiritual disciplines have to be cultivated and practiced intentionally and consistently to become regular rhythms and/or postures in our lives and to have heart-changing effects.

This Phase will deepen your understanding of the workplace as a primary location for discipleship, and of some of the spiritual postures, practices, and disciplines that are needed in and alongside our work to direct our hearts towards the kingdom.

Reflections

▶ WATCH (2 MINUTES)

Let's watch two business leaders and a theologian reflect on the necessity of being attentive to matters of spiritual formation at work

Phase 5 Video 1: Chi En Yu (1:08)

Phase 5 Video 2: Eric Stumburg (0:44)

💬 DISCUSS (15 MINUTES)

- Do you ever catch yourself making decisions to earn money without regard for the cost? If so, how might that be forming or malforming you?

- Do you think about your work as *your* work? What would it take for you to think about work as *God's* work and how might that form you differently?

Going Deeper (10 minutes)

▶ WATCH (4 MINUTES)

Phase 5 Video 3: "Work as Formation" – Mike Langford (3:28)

💬 DISCUSS (6 MINUTES)

- Do you believe God is already at your work? Why or why not?

- If in fact, God is present in mundane, invisible work like washing pots and pans, how can we make ourselves more aware of him in the midst of our own work?

Story: Bellmont Cabinets

"God kept saying, 'Do you trust me?'"

📖 READ

Steve Bell is an award-winning entrepreneur and CEO of Bellmont Cabinets. Let's watch a story about how two severe downturns acted as significant parts of his spiritual journey and formation.

▶ WATCH (8 MINUTES)

Phase 5 Video 4: "God Loves Cabinets"

💬 DISCUSS (20 MINUTES)

- What do you think of Steve's story? Where was God during the downturns?

- What challenges have you experienced in your work life? Have you ever wondered where God was during those times? How did God use those difficult times in your life?

- Even though faithfulness doesn't necessarily mean material blessing, our work gives us an opportunity to life faithfully. What can you do to live faithfully in your work context?

While Bellmont is currently thriving, the message of the story is not that faithfulness will be rewarded with material blessings (profit), but that God is with us, even in our suffering. In fact, suffering is often good for the formation of our souls. Steve is someone who has been very intentional in how he runs his business and introspective about how business has formed him spiritually, especially through suffering and learning to trust God in difficult times.

He is also a very intentional practitioner of the spiritual disciplines – he sees his work as worship and as a vessel for grace. He also begins each morning with prayer and Scripture reading, gives and volunteers regularly, and has built a culture of giving and community service at his company.

 PRAY/JOURNAL (10 MINUTES)

Heavenly Father, thank you for the work you have done in Steve Bell's life. Thank you for the journeys you have given all of us and for your constancy as we navigate the good times and the bad. May you continue to guide my journey and provide opportunities to live out my spiritual formation in my work life. Amen.

Going Deeper

📖 READ

Spiritual Practices/Disciplines and Postures

Like the trials Steve Bell faced, there are many opportunities for spiritual growth woven into our daily routines, especially if we are attentive and open to them. However, we also need intentional disciplines, practices, and postures to allow room for the Holy Spirit to work in our lives.

Spiritual practices (often called "disciplines") are critical to soul/heart formation. Richard Foster describes them as the narrow path to inner transformation. They navigate the middle ground between anti-nomianism (doing nothing) and striving. As such, they should be seen as *training* as opposed to *trying* to activate God's grace. Seattle Pacific University Provost Jeff Van Duzer states "they do not make God act any more than raising the sail on a boat causes the boat to move. But, they make us ready to receive the wind of the Spirit when it blows where it pleases (Jn 3:8)."

Spiritual disciplines that have been taught and practiced through church history include prayer, scripture study, generosity, solitude, worship, service, and celebration.

The short videos that follow introduce some spiritual disciplines, practices, and postures that seem especially important for business people. Not meant to be an exhaustive list, they focus on: dependence upon God, ceasing/Sabbath, solitude, and redemptive suffering. All act as partial antidotes to mal-formational stories and practices in business (work idolatry, control, greed/money) that can ensnare our hearts and direct us away from Christ.

Further Reflections

▶ WATCH (8 MINUTES)

To learn more about spiritual practices in and alongside our work, watch all or a selection of these "Thinking out Loud" videos:

Phase 5 Video 5: Mike Langford Pt. 2 (1:50)

Phase 5 Video 6: Chi-Ming Chien (1:47)

Phase 5 Video 7: Mike Bruce (1:48)

Phase 5 Video 8: Hans Hess (2:03)

‖–‖ EXERCISE

Business has its own cultural stories that compete with the biblical story for our allegiance, and aim to tell us what's ultimately important, how we should prioritize our time, and how we should treat co-workers, subordinates, and customers. But unconsciously, adopting these stories and living into them can become mal-formational as they direct our hearts away from the kingdom.

Describe some of the cultural stories (i.e., that profit is all important, our identity comes from what we do, customers are only means to more revenue) and/or practices (not revealing important information, checking messages as the first and last act of the day, overworking) that you regularly encounter and that have the potential to be mal-formational.

Then, describe some postures, practices, and disciplines you could incorporate into your day in order to acknowledge God's presence, cooperate with his efforts to transform you at work, and counteract the power of mal-formational cultural stories and practices.

_____

_____

_____

_____

Intentional and regular rhythms of spiritual disciplines, postures, and practices are critical in creating space for God to form us and prepare us to live vocationally integral lives.

If work has the power to shape us in subconscious ways, it's all the more important to integrate spiritual disciplines, practices and postures into your day.

As we see with Steve Bell and Bellmont Cabinets, God is with us in the good and the bad times. Intentional spiritual habits will help you trust God in the difficult times.

✏️ PRAY/JOURNAL

What will you change tomorrow to better tune your life toward spiritual formation?

_____

_____

_____

_____

_____

_____

Part 2: Right Relationships

The second part of this study focuses on right relationships in the marketplace. Based upon the foundations developed in Part 1, we will explore some of the implications of participating in God's mission of redeeming every corner of culture. In particular, we will focus on re-imagining relationships with employees, customers, communities, and creation.

Phase 6

The Workplace as a Redemptive Community

The Workplace as a Redemptive Community

Introduction (5 minutes)

Work is often approached as only an economic exchange. Employees diligently serve their organizations and, in return, they should receive fair wages and benefits. Yet if we are to take seriously God's deep love for people and concern for right relationships, work represents something more. Ideally, the workplace should be a key venue where employees get to live out their vocations and grow into their full potential as people.

Research and experience suggest, however, that this is often not the case. Many people have jobs that offer minimal levels of engagement, meaning, and purpose. As a result, they experience alienation from themselves, others, and God in their work.

This Phase explores what it means for a workplace to function as a redemptive community. We will explore characteristics of leaders and organizations that enable employees to flourish. The study of leadership and organizations is often conducted in service of getting more out of employees. However, the motivation for Christian employers should be to reflect God's love for people.

People Development

We can see employees as resources or the way God sees them – as eternal souls to be loved, served, and developed. Let's begin by watching short videos of business leaders and a subject matter expert, all expressing theologically informed thinking about redemptive workplaces.

Reflections

▶ WATCH (10 MINUTES)

Phase 6 Video 1: Bill Pollard (0:54)

Phase 6 Video 2: Emily Padula (1:45)

Phase 6 Video 3: Eric Stumberg (1:34)

Phase 6 Video 4: Denise Daniels (6:38)

💬 DISCUSS (20 MINUTES)

- Why do people get treated as resources rather than as souls to be loved and developed into the people God intends for them to be?

- What would change in your workplace if the effect on the lives of employees were a key metric?

- How might your workplace realistically change so that work is more developmental and meaningful for an employee?

Story: Misfit Wearables

"Business is the way I express the faith that I have and it cannot be separated from my life. Because of that, God has to be there."

📖 READ

To learn more about servant leadership and how it can be enacted in business, let's watch a short story film called "There and Enough" and a short "Thinking Out Loud" piece. They're both about a company called Misfit Wearables and its founders, Sonny Vu and Christy Trang Le, who have worked to model and embed servant leadership in the company's culture.

▶ WATCH (10 MINUTES)

Phase 6 Video 5: "There and Enough " (8:00)

Phase 6 Video 6: Sonny Vu (1:54)

💬 DISCUSS (15 MINUTES)

- Misfit is located in Vietnam and seeks to build community in the country where Sonny and Christy were born and that suffers from lack of opportunity. Where is your community and how can you use your work to better influence it?

- How can you practice servant leadership at work?

- If you are a supervisor, what steps can you take to make work more meaningful for employees?

Although the Bible never offers a direct treatise on leadership, it gives many examples of servant leadership. Jesus himself came to serve (Mk. 10:45; Jn 13: 14-15). Leading and serving frequently go hand in hand in Scripture (Mt. 23:11; II Cor. 4). Thus, the job of a leader isn't to boss people around, and/or squeeze more out of people, but to serve those they are called to lead.

Good leadership is a key enabler of redemptive workplaces. Leaders set the tone for how employees experience their work. In fact, about 50% (Gallup study 2015) of workers reportedly quit their jobs because of a poor relationship with their supervisor.

The Bible places a strong emphasis on mutuality, reconciliation, and right relationships in all of our dealings. Employees are called to work diligently and to respect those in power, while leaders have duties to serve those in their charge. Serving employees doesn't preclude holding them to high standards or redirecting them to other positions for justifiable reasons.

Heavenly Father, thank you for the work you are doing at Misfit Wearables. Thank you for the example of servant leadership Sonny and Christy display. May you inspire me to impart your values in my daily work to help me build relationships with everyone around me. Amen.

⊩⊩ EXERCISE

We have all experienced a variety of workplaces, likely some more enjoyable than others. What elements of the workplace contributed to your enjoyment of a specific job? What elements of the workplace degraded your job satisfaction?

Write down a list of must-haves for what you believe a redemptive workplace should look like.

_____

_____

_____

_____

_____

📖 READ

In addition to leadership and treating people as souls (vs. resources), generosity, fairness, and boundedness are other important Biblical concerns that are key characteristics of workplaces where people can flourish.

Going Deeper

Let's further explore how Christian theology can inform the design of good work and workplaces.

▶ WATCH (9 MINUTES)

Phase 6 Video 7: Chi-Ming Chien (3:08)

Phase 6 Video 8: Denise Daniels on Sabbath (2:45)

Phase 6 Video 9: Mike Bruce (1:36)

Phase 6 Video 10: Don Flow (1:54)

💬 DISCUSS (10 MINUTES)

- Which parts of redemptive workplaces are already present where you work? What can you do to keep these elements in place and/or expand them?

- What prevents your workplace from including these, or similar, considerations? How might including them change the culture of your workplace?

🔥 KEY TAKEAWAYS (7 MINUTES)

- Work is intended to be more than only an economic exchange of labor for wages, but an important means by which we can flourish, grow into, and express our full humanity.

- Created in the image of God, employees (as image bearers) should be loved as neighbors rather than seen as tools or resources. The question and practical importance of what/who people are becoming in their work is a central consideration. Work should be designed to be as developmental, meaningful, and bounded as possible.

- Leadership. The Bible places great emphasis on mutuality – we are called to promote reconciliation and right relationships in all our dealings. Leading and serving seem to go hand in hand in the Scriptures (i.e., Mt 23:11). Thus, we should look out for the best interests of our employees and co-workers.

How might I build relationships through my work context?

_____

_____

_____

_____

_____

_____

Customer Relationships:
Re-personalizing the Marketplace

Customer Relationships:
Re-personalizing the Marketplace

Introduction (5 minutes)

The nature of relationships with customers has changed greatly over time. Before the industrial revolution, goods and services were mostly made and sold within the confines of a local region. People produced as much as was needed for those around them. But when production outpaced local demand, the need to sell the excess (and thereby professionalized "marketing") to the larger community and even the globe became necessary.

The work of convincing someone to buy has always been loaded with the temptation to misrepresent. However, marketing messages and methods have evolved over the last century. Where early promotional messages focused on product features (brighter, faster, stronger, cleaner), new techniques take aim at the consumer's subconscious and use data collected from a wide range of sources to gain more leverage over purchase decisions. All sorts of marketing techniques are available to use to try to push consumer's buy buttons, without apparent regard for their well-being.

The marketplace has been deeply de-personalized. Efficient transactions have displaced lasting and respectful relationships. Instead of sealing a deal with eye contact, a firm handshake and well wishes, our goods often arrive with a thud on our porches and a quick door knock. Frequently, the only human connections are the sound of footsteps and a quick glimpse of a delivery person's back as they hustle back to their truck.

Amid these changes (and very real competitive challenges), can we re-personalize the marketplace, treat our customers as neighbors, and look out for their best interests? This module will explore the contours of a theology of customer relationships and marketing. We will consider ways that marketing and engaging with customers can be re-imagined in light of right relationships.

Reflections

Let's begin by watching short reflections by two business leaders.

▶ WATCH (1 MINUTE)

Phase 7 Video 1: Don Flow (0:27)

Phase 7 Video 2: Emily Padula (0:32)

- How might we go about re-personalizing (or more deeply personalizing) a business relationship?

- How has God served you during your Christian walk? In what ways could that experience help you serve others in business?

Story: Magpies

"We are never trying to sell anything. We are trying to connect; we are trying to know; we are trying to serve."

READ

Let's learn about a small retail business based out of Nashville, TN called Magpies. Owner Maggie Tucker has put significant thought and effort into loving and serving her customers.

WATCH: (6 MINUTES)

Phase 7 Video 3: "Girl, I Love You" (4:00)

Phase 7 Video 4: Maggie Tucker (2:00)

DISCUSS (15 MINUTES)

- How might you reimagine your marketing practices to better meet the needs of your customers as people made in God's image?

- You might say this approach only works in hands-on-related fields like retail, but how might a relational approach work in fields further removed from the end user?

- What should Christians do in industries where the product isn't as life affirming? For example, sugary soft drinks aren't very healthy. Should Christians market those products?

PRAY/JOURNAL (5 MINUTES)

Heavenly Father, thank you for the work of Maggie Tucker. Thank you for her call to love these girls right where they are rather than pushing them out of the "in between." Help me to think about the relationships around me and the customers I serve. Help me to love my customers and meet their needs so they can be who you have called them to be. Amen.

EXERCISE

Maggie clearly honors the personhood of her customers. They aren't targeted personas, nor are they measured by revenue potential; they are human beings possessing the wide range of experiences and emotions we all have.

Who are the customers around your business? Write down the people that come to mind and think about life in their shoes. Write down what they want and what will help them flourish.

_____

_____

_____

_____

_____

_____

A worldly view of marketing:

> Influencing people to buy things they don't really need, won't really use, and will throw away quickly just to buy the next thing they don't really need, won't really use, and will throw away quickly.

A theological view of marketing:

> Seeing customers as God sees them — as people to be known, loved, and served to facilitate mutually beneficial exchange.

Digging Deeper: Theology of Marketing

▶ WATCH (3 MINUTES)

> Phase 7 Video 5: Erik Lokkesmoe, "Theology of Marketing" (2:55)

💬 DISCUSS (10 MINUTES)

- What are key components of your theology of marketing? What are you committed to doing and not doing? How do you see your customers? How do you demonstrate concern for their best interests?

- How can you be more authentic in telling your story to customers?

Story: Love Made Visual at Apple

"Our Geniuses aren't repairing a computer; they are restoring a relationship."

📖 READ

Let's watch a short film about two former senior executives at a very well-known and beloved company, Apple. Both were hired by Steve Jobs and both were very intentional in bringing their faith to bear on their work in retail and sales.

▶ WATCH (7 MINUTES)

Phase 7 Video 6: "Faith at a $700b Company"

💬 DISCUSS (15 MINUTES)

- When we think about some of the largest businesses in the world, we often view them as soulless or uncaring of an average person, and yet Ron and John were able to instill their Christian values into their work. In what meaningful ways can you bring your values to work?

- How might your business development and sales process change to better make love visual?

✏️ PRAY/JOURNAL (5 MINUTES)

Heavenly Father, thank you for the work of Ron and John. Thank you for their thoughtfulness on how to love people in one of the largest businesses in the world. I pray that you can provide opportunities for me to love others through my work. Amen.

🏋 EXERCISE

Write down two things you can do tomorrow to love others through your work.

_____

_____

_____

_____

🔥 KEY TAKEAWAYS (5 MINUTES)

The Magpies and Apple stories show how marketing and re-imagining customer relationships can help people flourish. Even Apple, one of the largest companies in the world, can design its retail and sales experiences in a way to meet the needs of one person, and to build relationships in a lasting and loving way.

In light of God's redemptive work in the world, we can shift our view of marketing away from selling people things they don't need, won't use, and will throw away, to a position of mutually beneficial exchange through developing real and lasting relationships.

How might I use sales and marketing in my work context to best foster mutually beneficial exchange and the restoration of relationships?

_____

_____

_____

_____

_____

Phase 8

Business and Flourishing Communities

Business and Flourishing Communities

Introduction (5 minutes)

As we studied in Phase 3, the Fall affected all areas of life. People, communities, systems, and structures are all broken to various degrees, making life difficult even for those who make the right choices.

For many of us using this study guide, poverty is likely an abstract concept. Our society has worked diligently to hide the symbols and symptoms of economic impoverishment. The entertainment we consume often focuses on affluent characters struggling with rich-world problems.

Many of us try to "keep up with the Joneses." We look to those who have a little bit more than we do and aspire to attain similar life styles. We may even make educational and career choices to move up the ladder: the bigger house, the fancier car. But many business-minded people living in wealthy countries are already on the highest rungs.

In sharp contrast, it's not unusual to see poverty alongside visual symbols of booming economic growth in wealthy countries like the U.S. Across the globe, a few billion people still struggle to get by on just a few dollars per day, which means poor nutrition, sanitation, and lack of access to medications for deadly but treatable diseases. The sheer number of people living on the margins is a sharp contrast to the vision of Shalom portrayed in the Bible.

While we often think that fighting poverty is the responsibility of governments and NGOs, the Bible states that we all have roles to play. For example, farmers in the Old Testament (business people in their day) were to leave the edges of their fields unharvested for poor people to glean.

Moving beyond employees and customers, how can today's Christian business people be good neighbors and help their local and/or global communities flourish? In addition to charity, how can businesses *intentionally* leverage their unique resources to improve the lives of people who are marginalized?

This phase will explore Biblical teaching on poverty, our response and how business can help. We will learn about some faith-motivated entrepreneurs who are working to create economic opportunities for marginalized people through profit earning businesses.

Story: Verdant Frontiers

"If you are a thief, quit stealing. Instead, use your hands for good hard work, and then give generously to others in need." Ephesians 4:28

📖 READ

Let's watch a short film about Scott Friesen, a successful entrepreneur who achieved his aim of personal wealth, but whose encounter with Christ has led him to very different objectives in his current work.

▶ WATCH (4 MINUTES)

Phase 8 Video 1: "All In"

💬 DISCUSS (10 MINUTES)

- Scott talks about gainful employment as a life-changing experience. How have you felt in those times of unemployment and under-employment? Are there ways for you, in your current work context, to make a difference for those in unemployed or under-employed circumstances?

- Verde Beef invests in Ethiopian communities. Are there opportunities for you to invest in communities outside of your own, the ones most in need? What would such an investment look like?

- What advantages and/or disadvantages does enlisting business in the fight against poverty have over traditional forms of charity or aid? What could go wrong in doing business with vulnerable people? Could the profit motive lead to mission drift and/or exploitative practices to meet return expectations of investors?

✏️ PRAY/JOURNAL (5 MINUTES)

Heavenly Father, thank you for the call you have placed on Scott's life. Thank you for the transformational work you have done to transition the view of people from a means to an end. Thank you for Verdant Frontiers and the work it does in Ethiopia. May you help me to think about my work globally and to consider ways my work can make a difference not only here, but also in other places around the world. Amen.

Going Deeper: Biblical Teaching on Poverty

📖 READ (5 MINUTES)

While poverty is typically understood as the lack of material wealth, the Bible portrays it in multi-dimensional terms – the lack of economic, social, relational, emotional and/or spiritual well-being (i.e., "man does not live on bread alone"- Mt. 4:4).

The point here isn't to trivialize economic poverty and the suffering that comes with it, but to recognize that we are all poor in some way, so we have no reason to feel superior to those who have fewer financial resources than we do. In fact, those who are economically poor often have greater levels of spiritual maturity because they have to rely on God for their daily needs.

The Bible also states that caring for the economically poor is fulfillment of the gospel, not optional to it (see Lk. 4:18-19). In other words, it's a matter of justice and not just charity. In fact, Scripture portrays our response to those in need as a critical test of our spiritual maturity (Is. 58:10; James 2:15-17). We cannot be in right relationship with God unless we are demonstrating care for those who are economically disadvantaged (Ex. 23:11; Deut. 15:11)

Story: Dayspring Technologies

📖 READ

While global poverty captures our attention, we don't need to travel far to join God's work of loving our neighbors. Originally formed to help create opportunities (technology training) for underserved youth in San Francisco, the leaders of this organization have given lots of thought to what it means to be committed to a faithful vision of biblical hospitality to their neighbors.

▶ WATCH (9 MINUTES)

> Phase 8 Video 2: "Dayspring (Monastery 2.0)"

💬 DISCUSS (15 MINUTES)

- What do you think of Dayspring's move to the Bayview neighborhood and the ways the company's employees go about trying to be good neighbors?

- Dayspring shares its office space with Redeemer Community Church. What do you think about that partnership? How can businesses and churches better partner to meet the needs of local communities?

- Some of Dayspring's offerings might not make much money, but they do it because it's the right thing to do. Are there products or offerings your company could provide, even if they don't offer the highest margins? How might you navigate the tension between meeting the needs of others and remaining a profitable business?

✎ PRAY/JOURNAL (5 MINUTES)

Heavenly Father, thank you for the vision you have given Dayspring Technologies to use its skills and treasures to make a difference in their community. Thank you for the relationships that you are building. Thank you for the difference you have made in the work of Yvonne and her bakery. I pray that you would open my eyes to those in need in my immediate community. May I build relationship and seek to serve in whatever ways are possible. Amen.

Dayspring Technologies works to meet the needs of people in its community. The Neighbor Fund began with Chi-Ming Chien walking around during his sabbatical. The project began because someone decided to be present and to intentionally build relationship. What steps can you take to build relationships with people in your community?

_____

_____

_____

_____

_____

Story: I Have a Bean

"We have employees that because they have a label of felon are seen by society as being in the bottom 1% from a human quality standpoint, but here they are producing product rated in the top 1%. We are doing that so the quality of their work will change the perception of the public."

📖 READ

While many of us embrace creating opportunities for those who lack them through no fault of their own, we may not feel the same way about those who have made poor choices. Yet the Gospel is about second chances. Let's hear the story of a small business located near Chicago. *I Have a Bean* is dedicated to hiring individuals recently released from prison as an expression of participation in God's redemptive mission through elevating people so that others can see them the way God sees them.

▶ WATCH (8 MINUTES)

Phase 8 Video 3: "The Top 1%"

💬 DISCUSS (15 MINUTES)

- Pete saw the need to create redemptive opportunities for people who were shunned by society. In what ways can you imprint redemption into the relationships you have at work?

While we aren't all called to create jobs for those returning from prison, the Bible teaches that how we treat those who are voiceless and invisible in our own communities or organizations is a test of our faith. So how can we be more intentional in creating opportunities and/or giving dignity and voice to those in or outside of our organizations who, for whatever reason, lack them?

Pete had two epiphanies: the appreciation of good coffee and (through the experience of a family member who was unemployable after committing a crime), the need to create redemptive opportunities for people who were shunned by society. Pete's employees and the top-quality coffee they produce make us confront assumptions we have about people who have been in prison.

✎ PRAY/JOURNAL (5 MINUTES)

Heavenly Father, thank you for Pete Leonard and the redemptive work of *I Have A Bean*. Thank you for the many lives the company has touched all in the name of making good coffee. I pray for the opportunities I have in my work and in the community around me. May I be intentional in giving dignity and a voice to those who lack such things. Amen.

Write down ways your work can intentional build up the community around you.

_____

_____

_____

_____

_____

Further Reflections (10 minutes, optional)

To learn more about how businesses are working to better the lives of vulnerable people, watch the following "Thinking Out Loud" videos:

Video 4: Dave Munson (2:47)

Video 5: Christy Tran Le (2:44)

Video 7: Pete Leonard (1:24)

Video 8: Greg Long (:49)

Video 9: David Flory (2:15)

Video 10 Emily Padula (1:34)

🔥 KEY TAKEAWAYS (5 MINUTES)

Poverty should never be an abstract concept. Those of us in positions of relative wealth and affluence have a mandate to restore relationships and enact justice. Through *Verdant Frontiers, Dayspring Technologies*, and *I Have a Bean*, we see organizations seeking to find ways toward the restoration of relationships through business activity. In each instance, a clear first step is to intentionally get to know people outside our bubble, understand what God is already doing, and then create strategies that sustainably help meet those needs.

Let's stop keeping up and instead consider ways we can practice lifting up others.

- An important way that business can participate in the mission of God is by leveraging its unique and indispensable talents and resources to help alleviate poverty.

- While business acting as business already contributes to the common good, much can be done for the sake of poverty and injustice in the world through intentional efforts.

- Business people can be agents of justice/shalom in many different ways within their spheres of influence.

How might I make a real difference to issues of poverty through my work?

_____

_____

_____

_____

_____

_____

Business and the Environment

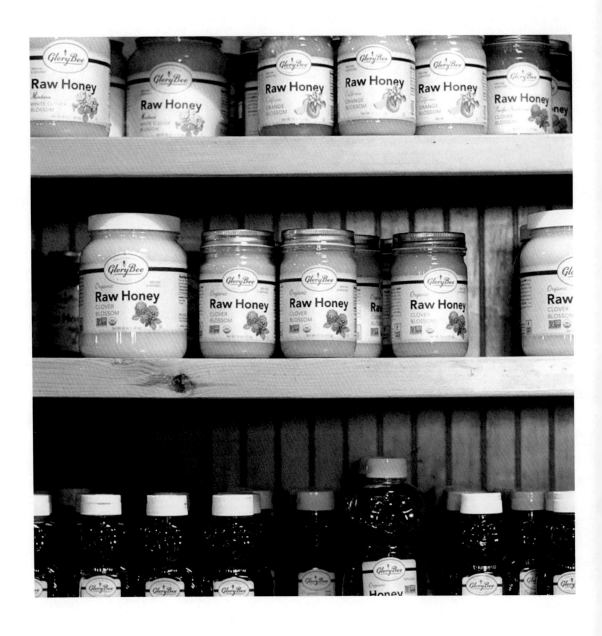

PHASE 9

Business and the Environment

Introduction (5 minutes)

A famous megachurch pastor infamously caused a scandal in Christian circles a few years ago when he took the stage and told conference attendees that he proudly drives a gas-guzzling SUV because in his understanding of the Bible, the whole world is going to burn up in the future anyway.

For many years, this view – although not so brazenly stated — has permeated large parts of the Christian community. Until recently, many Christians haven't been too concerned about the environment. Some still aren't. Behind their apathy may be theological beliefs like:

- God only cares about saving souls, so the material world doesn't matter to him.

- God gave us dominion over the earth, so we can use it as we see fit.

- When Jesus returns, the world will be destroyed and a new one will be created, so why take care of it when there are souls that need saving?

But does the Bible actually teach these positions? What if the environment is more integral to God's redemptive agenda than some traditional views hold?

Beyond clear cases of abuse, what responsibilities do Christian business people have for the well-being of the environment? *Every* business simultaneously depends upon and affects the environment while providing goods and/or services (through sourcing, manufacturing, packaging, delivery and disposal). What priority should environmental considerations receive amid competing obligations such as job creation, greater efficiency, or less expensive products?

This Phase will re-examine Biblical teaching on creation and some implications for the roles of business.

Story: Elevation Burger

"Should Christians care about the environment? Absolutely. We were created in an environment. And that environment was given to us."

📖 **READ**

Hans Hess is an entrepreneur who is motivated by a deep sense of calling to operate businesses in ways that are faithful to the whole gospel by promoting human and environmental health.

▶ **WATCH (6 MINUTES)**

Phase 9 Video 1: "Elevation"

💬 **DISCUSS (15 MINUTES)**

- Hans' beliefs about environmental responsibility and its integral relationship with human well-being are far different than a narrow interpretation of dominion as irresponsible use. How do you view and biblically ground a Christian's responsibilities toward creation?

- You might watch this video and appreciate that Hans is trying to make hamburgers healthier for people and the environment, but think, "They are still hamburgers." How healthy is healthy? Is it important to make bad things less bad? Or should Christians work toward even more restorative diets?

- Is the environment solely the responsibility of business? What roles do governments and consumers need to play?

✏️ **PRAY/JOURNAL (5 MINUTES)**

Heavenly Father, thank you for the vision you have given to Hans Hess to make hamburgers in a more healthy and sustainable way. Thank you for the environment you have given us. May we find ways to steward it well in advance of the future day when we all sit down together at the marriage supper of the Lamb. May my actions benefit the environment around me. Amen.

🏋 **EXERCISE**

What changes can your business make to enact better care for creation?

_____

_____

_____

_____

_____

Going Deeper: Biblical Teaching on the Environment

▶ **WATCH (6 MINUTES)**

Phase 9 Video 2: Dr. JJ Johnson Leese

Let's explore Biblical teaching on the environment by turning to a subject matter expert, Dr. JJ Johnson Leese. Dr. Johnson Leese is a theology professor at Seattle Pacific University, the author of a recent book on environmental theology and the co-owner (with her husband, Bill) of a fishing business in Alaska.

💬 DISCUSS (10 MINUTES)

- How does Dr. Johnson Leese's interpretation of the Bible differ from traditional understandings of Scripture's teaching on environmental responsibility?

- What does the final imagery of a city in Revelation mean for our work and its relationship to sustainability?

Story: GloryBee

"Bees are incredible creatures. I can't help but look at a bee and realize that there's got to be a God."

📖 READ

Let's watch a short film about a family owned-business operating out of Eugene Oregon, GloryBee. The owners have long been committed to environmental sustainability and to the health and well-being of the customers and community.

▶ WATCH (10 MINUTES)

Phase 9 Video 3: "GloryBee"

💬 DISCUSS (15 MINUTES)

- Sustainability practices make sense given GloryBee's industry (bees make honey, a key product line), but how might such initiatives gain support in less relevant industries?

- How important is environmental stewardship in your work context? What changes could your business make to measure and track its environmental stewardship?

✏️ PRAY/JOURNAL (5 MINUTES)

Heavenly Father, thank you for the work of the Turanski family and GloryBee Products. Thank you for the passion they have for the honey bee and for the work they are doing to save the honey bee. I pray that I can take a position of stewardship in my daily life. May you give me the opportunity to make environmentally conscious decisions. Amen

⊪–⊩ EXERCISE (5 MINUTES)

- GloryBee is a certified B-Corp, a designation that requires rigorous reporting on standards and metrics. Any solution to environmental sustainability requires partnerships between business, government, and individuals.

- Write down some strategies for how you could start to build those relationships in your community.

_____

_____

_____

_____

Further Reflections (10 minutes, optional)

To learn more about how businesses are engaging in creation care, watch a selection of the following "Thinking Out Loud" videos:

Video 4: Dave Munson (2:07)

Video 5 David Flory (:43)

Video 6 Hans Hess (2:10)

Video 7 Dick and Pat Turanski (:36)

Video 8 Scott Friesen (1:18)

Video 9: Rae Jean Wilson (2:03)

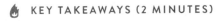 KEY TAKEAWAYS (2 MINUTES)

Having encountered a different understanding of the end of the world and the stories of Elevation Burger and GloryBee, our attitudes and actions toward creation matter greatly. Unlike the pastor who boasted to conference attendees, maybe we should consider the car we drive and our business practices. If the environment is similar to a house in which we get to live for a few years, we would respect the owner's wishes and try our best to leave it in a better state than when we arrived. So why should the environment be any different?

Creation care means:

- The belief that the Bible supports environmental neglect or degradation is erroneous.

- The Bible can be understood in a way that strongly supports creation care as a key part of God's redemptive agenda.

- Business should be conducted in a manner in which care for God's creation is a significant consideration/another bottom line.

- The well-being of the environment is not solely the responsibility of business. Consumers and governments also play important roles.

Phase 10

Next Steps

Next Steps

Summary (20 minutes)

During these past 9 weeks, we've affirmed business as a calling and developed a Biblical framework with implications for why and how we should go about our work.

So far, we've covered:

Foundations

Phase 1: Introduction to the Study

Phase 2: Business as a Calling

Phase 3: Business in the Messy Middle

Phase 4: Ethics and Core Values

Phase 5: Spiritual Formation

Right Relationships

Phase 6: The Workplace as a Redemptive Community

Phase 7: Customers: Re-Personalizing the Marketplace

Phase 8: Business and Flourishing Communities

Phase 9: Creation Care

💬 DISCUSS

- What were the highlights of the study? Describe a few key takeaways.

- What were the most challenging themes from the course? What will you try to change?

- What questions remain?

NEXT STEPS (60 MINUTES)

Hopefully, the past 10 weeks have inspired you to make concerted efforts toward instilling vocation into your business journey. But, if we all just stop here, we may never see God's call for business on purpose in action.

No matter your role and business context, a plan of action is required to move from the theoretical to the practical. So for the majority of this concluding section, based upon what you have learned, map out where you would like to be one week, one month, three months, and six months from now. Be practical and specific. Keep in mind that God is already present at your work, so some aspects of it are worth affirming and celebrating.

If it's helpful, frame your responses using the S.M.A.R.T. framing device for setting goals. You know you've set an accurate goal when it is:

- **Specific:** Your goals need to be clear so you can have a guiding "north star." Know what you are trying to accomplish, what resources it will take to do it, how many people you need to collaborate with, etc. Don't assume anything.

- **Measurable:** Your goals need to be quantifiable in order to track your progress. Is there a way to answer how much, how many, or otherwise how you will know you have accomplished it?

- **Achievable:** A goal like alleviating poverty and/or injustice isn't specific enough. Committing to raising wages and/or investing specific dollar amounts to serve low income communities is.

- **Results-Focused:** Your goals need to focus on the outcomes, not activities. Your goals need to be able to answer the changes you want to see in the world, not just the actions you plan to take.

- **Time-bound:** Your goals need to have deadlines. The exercise below helps frame what you are trying to do within specific timeframes. Think about what is truly achievable within those timeframes and commit to accomplishing your plan of action.

What does God's calling on your work look like one week from now?

_____

_____

_____

_____

What does God's calling on your work look like one month from now?

_____

_____

_____

_____

What does God's calling on your work look like three months from now?

_____

_____

_____

_____

_____

What does God's calling on your work look like six months from now?

_____

_____

_____

_____

_____

COMMISSIONING PRAYER (10 MINUTES)

Spend some time praying for and commissioning each other to the noble calling of joining in God's work of redeeming all corners of creation, including the messy, complicated marketplace.

Almighty God, we praise you, we give you our thanks for your grace toward us in Jesus Christ, through whom we have life, hope, and purpose.

We thank you for the gifts of service that you by your Holy Spirit have given to all your people, so that we may each serve you, and serve others.

We thank you for the call you have placed on all of us to live purposefully in the marketplace. May our lives be a reflection of you no matter our work context.

We pray that you may equip and empower us for ongoing service through our work.

May our work be worshipful to you. May we be purposeful in building relationships with our fellow workers, with our customers, and with the community at large.

May our actions align with the humble attitude of servanthood.

Thank you for the promises you have given us in Scripture. May we continue to build community in your name.

For we pray in Jesus' name, AMEN.

People

Cast Members:

Bruce Baker, Seattle Pacific University, Associate Professor of Business Ethics

Steve Bell, Bellmont Cabinets, CEO

John Brandon, Apple, Inc., VP, International (retired)

Mike Bruce, Inscope International, Founder and CEO

Chi-Ming Chien, Dayspring Technologies, Principal

Denise Daniels, Seattle Pacific University, Professor of Management

David Flory, Powerfield Solar, LLC, Managing Partner

Don Flow, Flow Companies, Inc., Chairman and CEO

Scott Friesen, Verdant Frontiers, Co-Founder

Steve Garber, Washington Institute for Faith, Vocation & Culture, Founder and Principal

Hans Hess, Elevation Burger, Founder & Chairman

Ron Johnson, Enjoy, CEO

JJ Johnson Leese, Seattle Pacific University, Assistant Professor of Theology

Mike Langford, Seattle Pacific University, Associate Professor of Theology

Pete Leonard, I Have a Bean, Founder and Roastmaster

Christy Trang Le, Misfit Wearables, COO

Erik Lokkesmoe, Aspiration Studios, Producer

Greg Long, GloryBee, Marketing and Communications

Ashley Marsh, Marsh Collective, Proprietor

Dave Munson, Saddleback Leather Company, Founder and Owner

Suzette Munson, Love 41, Founder and Owner

Marta Norton Klock, Morningstar Investment Management, LLC, Portfolio Manager

Emily Padula, Hill Country Memorial, Chief Strategy Officer

C. William Pollard, Fairwyn Investment Company, Chairman

Eric Stumberg, Tengo Internet, Founder & CEO

Maggie Tucker, Magpies, Founder & CEO

Alan Turanski, GloryBee, CEO

Jeff Van Duzer, Seattle Pacific University, Provost

Sonny Vu, Misfit Wearables, CEO and Director

Chi-En Yu, Dayspring Technologies, Mobile Strategist

Crew:

Executive Producers: Eric & Keri Stumberg, Gene Kim, Ross Stewart, Kenman Wong

Producer: Kenman Wong

Director of Digital Learning and Innovation: Rolin Moe

Directors (film): Sean Dimond & John Harrison (UNTAMED)

Assistant Producers: Dana Meaux & Isabelle Woodward

Content: Kenman Wong, Bruce Baker, Randy Franz, Mike Langford, Isabelle Woodward

Advisors: Mark Mayhew, Uli Chi, Al Erisman

Resources

Foundational books:

Jeff Van Duzer, *Why Business Matter to God (and What still Needs to be Fixed)* IVP, 2010.

Kenman Wong and Scott Rae. *Business for the Common Good: A Christian Vision for the Marketplace.* IVP Academic, 2011.

Organizations/Networks:

Center for Faith & Work (founded by Redeemer Church, NY): https://faithand-work.com/

Denver Institute for Faith and Work: https://denverinstitute.org/

DePree Center at Fuller Seminary: https://depree.org/

Ethix Magazine (Published by SPU's Center for Integrity in Business): http://blog.spu.edu/ethix/

Faith Driven Entrepreneur: https://www.faithdrivenentrepreneur.org/

Letourneau University Center for Faith and Work: http://centerforfaithandwork.com/

Made to Flourish (a pastors network on faith and work): https://www.madeto-flourish.org/

Nashville Institute for Faith and Work: https://www.nifw.org/

Praxis: http://www.praxislabs.org/

Regent College, Canada Reframe Course (small group curriculum on the Christian story and its implications for all of life): https://marketplace.regent-college.edu/Reframe

Theology of Work project (An extensive repository of Biblical commentary and essays on the theology of work): https://www.theologyofwork.org/

Recommended Books and Articles:

Helen Alford and Michael Naughton. *Managing as if Faith Mattered: Christian Social Principles in the Modern Organization.* University of Notre Dame Press, 2001.

Dorothy Bass, ed. *Practicing our Faith: A Way of Life for a Searching People.*

Dorothy Bass. *Receiving the Day: Christian Practices for Opening the Gift of Time.*

Dave Blanchard. "Frontiers of Faith and Entrepreneurship." *Medium.* Feb. 17, 2017. https://medium.com/@dave_blanchard/frontiers-in-faith-and-entrepreneurship-cultivating-an-alternative-imagination-27b21350a5a2

Christen Borgman Yates. "The Oxymoron of Proximate Justice." *Comment.* March 7, 2008.: https://www.theologicalhorizons.org/theological-horizons/2017/5/10/the-oxymoron-of-proximate-justice-christen-borgman-yates

Walter Bruggeman. *Sabbath as Resistance: Saying No to the Culture of Now.*

Michael Cafferky. *Business Ethics in Biblical Perspective.* IVP Academic, 2015.

Steve Corbett and Brian Fikkert, *When Helping Hurts.* Moody Publishers (new ed.), 2014.

Darrell Cosden. *The Heavenly Good of Earthly Work.* Baker Academic, 2006.

Ken Costa. *God at Work.* Thomas Nelson (reprint edition), 2016.

Andy Crouch. *Culture Making.* IVP, 2013.

Marva Dawn. *Keeping the Sabbath Wholly.* Eerdmans, 1989.

Calvin DeWitt. *Earthwise.* Faith Alive (3rd ed.), 2011.

Margaret Diddams, et al. "Implications of Biblical Rhythms and Rest for Organizational Practices" *Christian Scholars Review.*

Ken Eldred. *God is at Work: Transforming People and Nations through Business.* Regal Books, 2005.

Albert Erisman. "Bringing Meaning to Work: An Interview with Barry Rowan": Ethix. https://ethix.org/2011/07/27/telecommunications-barry-rowan

Albert Erisman. *The Accidental Executive: Lessons on Business, Faith & Calling from the Life of Joseph.* Hendrickson, 2015.

Richard Foster. *Celebration of Discipline.* Harper One, 1988.

Richard Foster. *The Challenge of the Disciplined Life.* Harper One, 1989.

John Gage. "Christians Working in the Messy Middle." *Washington Institute for Faith, Vocation & Culture.* March 15, 2012. http://www.washingtoninst.org/1733/christian-work-in-the-messy-middle/

Steve Garber. "Making Peace with Proximate Justice." *Comment.* December 1, 2007 : https://www.cardus.ca/comment/article/13/proximate-justice-a-symposium-on-christian-realism/

Steve Garber. *Visions of Vocation: Common Grace for the Common Good.* IVP, 2014.

Steve Garber. "Vocation Needs no Justification" *Comment.* Fall, 2010.

David Gill. "Upgrading the Ethical Decision Making for Business." *Business and Professional Ethics Journal.* 23 (4) 2004.

Joel Green. "Cultivating the Practice of Reading Scripture." *Catalyst.* Feb. 5, 2014. http://www.catalystresources.org/cultivating-the-practice-of-reading-scripture/

Oz Guinness. *The Call: Finding and Fulfilling the Central Purpose of Your Life.* Thomas Nelson, 2003.

Julia Hanna. "Meet P. Diddy's CFO." *Harvard Business School Working Knowledge,* June 14, 2004. https://hbswk.hbs.edu/archive/meet-p-diddy-s-cfo

Lee Hardy. *The Fabric of This World: Inquiries into Calling, Career Choice and the Design of Human Work.* Eerdmanns, 1990.

Abraham Heschel. *The Sabbath.* Farrar, Strauss & Giroux, 1975.

Richard Higginson. *Called to Account.* Eagle. 1993.

Richard Higginson. *Questions of Business Life: Workplace Issues from a Christian Perspective.* Authentic, 2002.

Alec Hill. *Just Business. Christian Ethics for the Marketplace.* (3rd Edition). IVP, 2018.

David Horrell. *The Bible and the Environment.* Routledge, 2014.

C. Neal Johnson. *Business as Mission.* IVP Academic. 2010.

JJ Johnson Leese. *Christ, Creation and the Cosmic Goal of Redemption.* T&T Clark, 2018.

Tim Keller and Katherine Leary Alsdorf. *Every Good Endeavor: Connecting your Work to God's Work.* Penguin Books, 2014.

Douglas Koskela. *Calling & Clarity.* Eerdmanns, 2015.

John Marsh. "The Resurrection of Place." *The Washington Institute of Faith, Vocation & Culture.* April 22, 2014. http://www.washingtoninst.org/7843/resurrection-of-place/

Mark Meehan. "Business is Mission." *Comment*. July 2, 2010.

Laura Nash. *Believers in Business*. Thomas Nelson, 1994.

Laura Nash and Scott McClennan. *Church on Sunday, Work on Monday*. Jossey-Bass. 2001.

Tom Nelson. *Work Matters: Connecting Sunday Worship to Monday Work*. Crossway, 2011.

Michael Novak. *Business as a Calling*. Free Press, 1993.

Fred Oakes. "Spiritual Formation in the Workplace": http://www.patheos.com/blogs/missionwork/2014/04/spiritual-formation-in-the-workplace-a-post-from-the-kern-pastors-network-director/

Scott Rae and Kenman Wong. *Beyond Integrity (3rd Edition)*. Zondervan, 2012.

Renovare, "Spiritual Disciplines." https://renovare.org/about/ideas/spiritual-disciplines

Steve Rundle and Tom Steffen. *Great Commission Companies*. IVP, 2011.

Doug Seebeck and Tom Stoner. *My Business, My Mission: Fighting Poverty through Partnerships*. Faith Alive, 2009.

Mark Sheerin. "Why I left World Vision for Finance." *Christianity Today*. *This is our City*. February 22, 2013. https://www.christianitytoday.com/thisisourcity/7thcity/why-i-left-world-vision-for-finance.html

Amy Sherman. *Kingdom Calling: Vocational Stewardship for the Common Good*. IVP 2011.

James K.A. Smith. *Desiring the Kingdom*. Baker Academic, 2009.

William Spohn. *Go and Do Likewise: Jesus and Ethics*. Continuum, 2000.

R.C. Sproul. *Stronger than Steel: The Wayne Alderson Story*. Harper & Row, 1980.

Max Stackhouse et al. *On Moral Business*. Eerdmans, 1995.

R. Paul Stevens. *Doing God's Business: Meaning and Motivation for the Marketplace*. Eerdmanns, 2006.

R. Paul Stevens. *The Other Six Days: Vocation, Work and Ministry in Biblical Perspective*. Eerdmanns, 2000.

The High Calling. "Everything Feels Like Failure When You Are in the Middle." https://www.theologyofwork.org/the-high-calling/blog/everything-feels-failure-when-you-are-middle

Theology of Work Project. "God's Presence in our Struggles at Work": https://www.theologyofwork.org/old-testament/psalms-and-work/book-1-psalms-141/gods-presence-in-our-struggles-at-work-psalm-23

Theology of Work Project. "Systematic Presentation of Ethics" https://www.theologyofwork.org/key-topics/ethics/systematic-presentation-of-ethics

Theology of Work Project. "What are God's Rules? Is There a Command for Every Occasion?": https://www.theologyofwork.org/key-topics/ethics/systematic-presentation-of-ethics/different-approaches-to-ethics/the-command-approach-in-practice/what-are-gods-rules-is-there-a-command-for-every-occasion

Miraslov Volf. *Work in the Spirit: Toward a Theology of Work.* Wipf & Stock (reprint edition), 2001.

Samuel Wells. *Improvisation: The Drama of Christian Ethics.* Brazos Press, 2004.

Dallas Willard. *Renovation of the Heart.* Navpress, 2012.

Dallas Willard. "Spiritual Formation in Christ: A Perspective on What It Is and How it Might Be Done": http://www.dwillard.org/articles/artview.asp?artID=81

Dallas Willard. *The Spirit of the Disciplines.* Harper One (reprint ed.) 1999.

Made in the USA
San Bernardino, CA
04 February 2019